ELIZABETH RING

SLED DOGS

ARCTIC ATHLETES

GOOD DOGS!
THE MILLBROOK PRESS · BROOKFIELD, CONNECTICUT

6113716

FOR JACK,
RHODE ISLAND ATHLETE

Cover photo courtesy of Bill Hennefrund

Photos courtesy of Kent & Donna Dannen: pp. 3, 4, 10, 11,
13, 19, 20, 24; Bettmann Archive: p. 7; UPI/Bettmann: p. 15;
Wide World Photos: pp. 17, 23, 26, 28.

Library of Congress Cataloging-in-Publication Data

Ring, Elizabeth, 1920-
Sled dogs : arctic athletes / by Elizabeth Ring.
p.   cm. — (Good dogs!)
Includes bibliographical references and index.
Summary: Describes the various breeds of arctic dogs, and their
demanding training for the high-endurance sport of dogsled racing.
ISBN 1-56294-292-1 (lib. bdg.)
1. Sled dogs—Juvenile literature. 2. Dogsledding—Juvenile
literature. 3. Sled dog racing—Juvenile literature. 4. Dog
breeds—Arctic regions—Juvenile literature. [1. Sled dogs.
2. Sled dog racing. 3. Dog breeds.] I. Title. II. Series.
SF428.7.R56 1994
636.7'3—dc20   93-15663 CIP AC

Published by The Millbrook Press
2 Old New Milford Road
Brookfield, Connecticut 06804

SLED DOGS

A Siberian husky howls with impatience for the start of a dogsled race. Like wolves, huskies are howlers rather than barkers.

A half hour out of Crazyhorse Camp near Prudhoe Bay, north of the Arctic Circle, the dogsled sped over hard-packed snow. There was no hint of a coming storm. Then, without warning, the sled was swallowed up in cold, stinging fog—a swirling Alaskan "whiteout."

Slim Randles's dog team kept running. Tanya, a big silver-gray dog, and Wolf, her strong black-coated partner, were in the lead. Behind them ran eight other dogs, pulling the sled steadily along the slick trail. The man rode standing on the back of the sled's runners.

Randles, a newspaper reporter and experienced dogsled driver, had been in whiteouts before. When the icy fog swept down on the sled, he knew a snowstorm could follow. Then the storm hit. Blinding snow whooshed up, down, and from every side. The winds made the already below-zero temperature feel at least thirty degrees colder. Quickly, Randles turned the dogs back toward camp, hoping desperately that the team would get there before the blizzard got too bad.

"Hy-a-a-ah!" Randles yelled, urging the dogs to go faster.

Randles could feel his breath start to freeze on his face. In minutes, he could barely open his mouth to shout commands to Tanya and Wolf. It hardly mattered. How could he direct the dogs if he could not see a foot in front of him? All he could do was crouch down, cling to the driving bow of the sled, and trust that Tanya's and Wolf's "dog sense" would guide them back to camp.

The dogs plowed ahead. On and on they went through the raging storm and the fast-deepening snow. Randles became more and more certain that they were off track. It would not be the first time his team had lost its way.

Then, quite suddenly, the whole team stopped short. Randles could not believe his dogs would quit on him this way. He felt his way forward in the swirling snow until he reached the head of the column of dogs. Tanya, usually reliable, was furiously digging a hole in a snowbank, as if refusing to go a step farther.

Frantic, Randles yanked on Tanya's collar, to get her going. But she refused to stop digging. Then Randles looked up, peering through the whiteness. Right in front of him was a porch. His dogs had brought the sled straight to the camp door.

Randles thawed out indoors. The dogs needed no shelter. Unharnessed and tied down for the night, they all dug holes for themselves in the snow. They curled up into tight balls of fur. They looped their tails over their noses, shielding their lungs from the frigid air. Bedded down under a blanket of snow, the dogs were as snug as if they were housed in an igloo.

Arctic dogs like Tanya and Wolf have helped people through fierce arctic winters for thousands of years. When did these hardy dogs first join forces with humans? Nobody knows exactly. Historians think it may have been about four thousand years ago, among the Eskimos of Siberia.

All anyone knows for sure is that at some time arctic dogs became people's companions and partners. They pulled sleds

Arctic Eskimos used dogs to pull sleds, hunt game, and guard camps against wolves and bears.

and herded reindeer. They helped in hunting wild animals such as seals and polar bears. They guarded camps against wolves and bears. In summer, they hauled flat sleighs over the tundra (arctic soil) and trotted along riverbanks pulling boats up- and down-stream. At times they carried packs on their backs.

Eskimos of eastern Siberia, Alaska, Greenland, and the Canadian Arctic were all nomads at one time. They moved from one place to another instead of living in permanent villages. Dogs (some crossbred with wolves) accompanied the migrant tribes.

In time, arctic people came to depend for their lives on their dogs. The Eskimos matched their smartest and strongest dogs to breed smart, sturdy pups. They also bred dogs that were especially good at scenting and tracking seals, polar bears, and musk-oxen. Much later, when dogsled racing became a popular sport, the dogs were bred (by both Eskimos and other people) for speed as well as intelligence, strength, and endurance.

CHARACTERISTICS OF ARCTIC DOGS · Arctic dogs are different from most other breeds of dogs. Living in a harsh climate, they have adapted to the cold. Over the centuries they have become hardier than dogs that live where it is warmer. Many sled dogs spend their lives out of doors. Their double-layered coats protect them from the coldest temperatures.

Arctic dogs can walk easily on snow and ice. Their feet are wide and flat, like small snowshoes, with thick, tough pads and strong toenails. Hair that grows between their toes cushions their pads. Even so, nowadays, they are often fitted with canvas booties to protect their feet when they run on jagged ice.

Most arctic dogs are muscular, deep-chested, and about 24 inches (60 centimeters) high at the shoulders. They may weigh anywhere from 50 to 85 pounds (23 to 38 kilograms), sometimes more.

Like many other dogs, some arctic dogs seem to be extrasensitive to the world around them—as Tanya and Wolf showed in following the invisible trail back to camp. Could they sniff the trail? Did they have some sixth sense of direction?

Some dog experts say that a sled dog remembers a trail once it has learned a path. Whatever the reason, countless sled dogs have led their teams to safety when blinding blizzards have struck.

All sled dogs share the natural ability and the instinct, or urge, to pull loads. But, as in any breed and any dog family, each dog is an individual. Some dogs are smarter than others. One likes to work; another is lazy. One is a clown; another is scrappy. One is steady and calm; another is stubborn and headstrong—just as in a group of human beings!

For one reason or another, some sled dogs may fight with other dogs. But few fight with people. Most sled dogs are friendly, spirited dogs, especially gentle and playful with children. They are, in fact, good company for anyone who treats them with understanding and respect.

SLED-DOG BREEDS · Some people call all sled dogs "huskies" (from "esky," short for Eskimo). But there are differences. Today, there are "purebreds" (registered by the American Kennel Club, the United Kennel Club, and other kennel clubs) such as Alaskan malamutes, Siberian huskies, and Samoyeds. And there are many crosses of these breeds among Alaskan huskies and Eskimo dogs. There are also a few other breeds and mixed breeds that have taken up dogsledding.

*Alaskan malamute*s are large dogs, their color ranging from silver to black, with white markings on their faces, feet, bellies, and legs. Their double-layered fur has a coarse outer layer and a short, thick, fine undercoat. They have brown eyes and round-tipped ears. Their tails wave like plumes over their backs. They howl, like wolves, rather than bark. Sometimes they "sing" together—as wolves do.

The Malamute Eskimos of western Alaska bred these dogs to be big, strong, and hardy—able to go long distances on very little food. Malamutes are especially good in weight-pulling contests, or freight races.

The Alaskan malamute is a powerful dog whose body is insulated by two thick layers of fur.

Although Siberian huskies are smaller than other sled dogs, they are very strong. And they love to pull loads!

Siberian huskies, smaller than other sled dogs, may be white or a mixture of tan, gray, silver, or black, with markings around their faces and eyes. Their outercoats are smooth and thick over short, fine undercoats. They have either brown or blue eyes, and some are "odd-eyed"—with one brown and one blue eye. Their ears sit higher on their heads than malamutes' ears, and the tips stick straight up. They carry their tails over their backs. Like malamutes, they are howlers rather than barkers.

Siberian huskies, as you might suspect, come from Siberia. Their ancestors were first used as sled dogs, probably over three thousand years ago, by a tribe of people called the Chukchi.

Samoyeds can be cream-colored or light beige, but most are snow-white. Their fur, with its strong, harsh outercoat and soft, insulating undercoat, puffs out around their neck and shoulders. They have dark almond-shaped eyes and black lips that curve upward, making them look as if they are always smiling.

Samoyeds are named for the Samoyed people of Siberia, with whom the dogs lived for many hundreds of years. They are thought to be the oldest of sled-dog breeds.

Alaskan huskies (also called "Indian dogs") are often a mixture of malamutes, Siberians, Samoyeds, other breeds such as hounds, bird dogs, and sometimes wolves (the most likely ancestor of all dogs). They are usually taller than Siberians and lighter in weight than malamutes.

Eskimo dogs (also known as "village dogs") sometimes look like malamutes or Siberian huskies, but more often they look like mongrels. They are, in fact, a mixture of many breeds. That does not keep individual dogs from being excellent sled dogs—many of them made almost waterproof by the thick, oily undercoating of their fur.

One of the oldest of the sled-dog breeds, the Samoyed was developed by tribes in northern Siberia to herd reindeer.

Other sled dogs. "Any dog pulling a sled is a sled dog," says Frank Hall of Jackson, Michigan. He and his wife, Nettie, have been trainers and sled drivers for years. Frank Hall has also built over four thousand dogsleds. "Just about any dog can be taught to pull," the Halls say. "Saint Bernards do an excellent job just for fun. Some dogs are naturals; they simply enjoy working."

Chow chows, as well as Samoyeds and Siberian huskies, are used as sled dogs in Siberia and in western North America. Newfoundlands and Labrador retrievers pull sleds in the eastern Arctic. Chinook dogs, a New England breed, were part of Admiral Richard E. Byrd's 1928 expedition to the Antarctic. Standard poodles have competed in long sled-dog races.

DOGSLEDS · Nowadays, arctic life is very different from what it was in the old days. Instead of dogsleds, northern people use snowmobiles, cars with four-wheel drive, and airplanes. But there are still places where dogsleds can go that machines cannot, such as through narrow mountain passes and over steep ice ridges. Long ago, different kinds of dogsleds were developed. The earliest were made of whalebone or driftwood. Sometimes handlebars were made of reindeer antlers.

Canadians and Greenlanders created the plank sled, with two wide runners, for traveling in soft snow. In Siberia and Alaska, sleds with a basket-shaped frame and long, narrow runners were built for narrow trails and icy surfaces.

Today sleds are still made of strong wood (usually ash, oak, hickory, or birch). No hardware is used in making dogsleds.

Parts are tied together by thongs of rawhide, twine, or plastic, rather than fastened with nails or screws. Frank Hall, the Michigan sledmaker, uses braided plastic (polyethylene) rope. Sleds made in this way are flexible and not apt to break as the sled twists and bounces on uneven trails.

A musher drives his sled-dog team across the frozen plains in Alaska. Because their feet are wide and flat, arctic dogs can easily walk on snow and ice.

A "brush bow" on the front of a sled acts as a bumper. At the back of a sled, the driver, called a "musher" (from the French word *marcher*, meaning "to walk" or "to march"), stands on the runners. The musher hangs onto a "drive bow" and leans right or left to help guide the sled. Sleds usually carry only food and supplies, not people—though, at times, an injured person or dog might become a passenger.

"Freight" sleds, used for carrying heavy loads, are longer and wider than other sleds.

DOGSLED HITCHES · There are, as there have always been, several ways to hitch dogs to a sled. In a fan-shaped hitch, lines attached to each of six to ten dogs all meet at one point at the front of the sled. This fan formation is fine for traveling in wide, open spaces, but not on narrow trails.

For dogsledding on trails, a long, narrow formation is used. Usually, dogs are "gang-hitched" in pairs to a towline (called a gangline). The gangline, attached to the front of the sled, runs between the paired dogs. There are varieties of this kind of hitch, such as the "tandem hitch" where dogs are attached to each side of a gangline, but not in pairs.

Harnesses fit across the dogs' chests and shoulders and along their backs. A tugline (for pulling the sled) runs from each harness to the gangline. A neckline (to keep the dog from dodging off to the side) runs from each dog's collar to the gangline.

At the front of the team is the "lead dog." Lead dogs are usually the smartest and fastest dogs. They set the pace and steer the

Two huskies
work together
to lead this
gang-hitched
team. Behind
them are the
point dogs
and two sets
of swing dogs.
The wheel dogs
are positioned
directly in front
of the sled.

team at the musher's commands. Sometimes a pair of dogs, connected by a double neckline, leads the team.

Behind the lead dog is a pair of "point dogs" (in Alaska, called "swing dogs"). They help to steer by holding to the trail when the sled makes turns. They are followed by strong, steady "swing dogs" (called "team dogs" in Alaska). Last in line, harnessed just in front of the sled, are the "wheel dogs." These are usually the largest and strongest dogs. They help the musher control the sled.

SLED-DOG TRAINING · While sled dogs love to run and to pull, they must be trained for teamwork. Some drivers start training their sled dogs when the pups are a couple of months old; others start them even younger than that. Susan Butcher, breeder, trainer, and champion sled-dog racer, begins the moment her slim, long-legged Alaskan husky pups are born. She makes friends with the pups, holding them, talking gently to them (even singing to them). As they grow, she feeds, grooms, and plays with them every day.

By the time Butcher is ready to train her dogs, the pups trust her and are eager to do what she asks of them. Butcher believes that the friendship she has with her dogs is the key to her success in racing.

When a pup is about two months old, it starts wearing a collar and a harness with a rope dangling from it. Later, as the pup grows, a piece of wood or some other object is attached to the rope. Later still, the pup hauls heavier objects around. Pulling something around is all a game to the dog.

Samoyed puppies investigate the sled they will someday pull.

By the time a dog is five or six months old, it learns basic sled-dog commands (one at a time). To start a team, the driver yells, "Hike," or "Let's go." Except in the movies, you do not often hear the word "mush" as a command. Drivers, however, are regularly called "mushers."

"Easy" tells the dogs to slow down. "Gee" means to turn right, "haw" to turn left. To turn around on a trail the driver calls, "come gee" or "come haw." "Whoa," of course, means to stop.

A malamute puppy in training. Dragging the tire helps him
get used to the harness—and it's great exercise.

Teamwork training usually takes place when a dog is between six and eight months old. A first outing may be alongside an experienced lead dog. Sometimes several pups trot along with several older, trained dogs.

When pups first pull a sled, they run only short distances. Next, they pull light loads. As in any exercise program, the dogs build up their strength and endurance. Gradually they run longer distances and pull heavier loads.

Naturally, mushers must be in good condition, too. Driving a dogsled is much harder than driving a car or riding a bicycle. The musher either runs behind the sled, rides on the long runners, or pedals (as on a scooter or skateboard). Mushers frequently must help push a sled up a steep slope or over obstacles on a trail. And sometimes they must turn an overturned sled right side up—occasionally with the help of their wheel dogs. Mushers must also be able to endure long trips in extremely cold weather—all the while remaining patient with their dogs.

ARCTIC AND ANTARCTIC EXPEDITIONS · Some of the hardiest mushers and sled dogs have taken part in treks to the North and South poles. In 1986, an eight-member expedition co-led by U.S. explorer Will Steger took forty-nine dogs (arctic huskies and Canadian Eskimo dogs) and five dogsleds on an expedition from Ellesmere Island in Canada to the North Pole. Unlike other expeditions, the teams received no extra airplane drops of supplies along the way. The trekkers were on their own. It was the first such expedition since Robert E. Peary became the first person to reach the North Pole, in 1909.

For 478 miles (769 kilometers), in temperatures that sometimes reached -70 degrees Fahrenheit (-21 degrees Celsius), the teams traveled on smooth, glaring ice, over jagged ice, on harsh, grainy "corn" snow, and on frozen seawater where the ice bobbed like a water bed. The dogs were well cared for. Steger's expedition made frequent stops to rest and eat. As supplies were used up and sled loads lightened, dogs that were no longer needed were airlifted back to Ellesmere Island. Six team members and twenty-one dogs made the whole fifty-six-day trip to the "Top of the World."

In 1990, thirty-six dogs (crossbreeds of Siberian husky, malamute, and timber wolf) went with Steger on a 4,000-mile (6,400-kilometer) trek, this time across Antarctica at the "Bottom of the World." This was the first team to go all the way across the continent by dogsled.

On this trip men from five different countries (France, Britain, China, Japan, and the Soviet Union) accompanied Steger on a five-month international scientific expedition. Halfway across the continent, they passed the South Pole. It was the first expedition to get to this place by dogsled since Roald Amundsen of Norway became the first man to reach the South Pole in 1911.

The scientists recorded ozone levels, measured temperatures and wind speeds and sea currents, searched for pollutants, and made other tests. At the end of their journey, they agreed that Antarctica was an endangered continent and that international cooperation was needed to protect this important part of the world.

Will Steger, leader of the 1990 team of explorers that would be the first to cross Antarctica by dogsled, points out his route across the "Bottom of the World."

As useful as sled dogs were in polar exploration, dogs have since been banned from Antarctica. Scientists believe that dogs have spread diseases (such as canine distemper) among seals and other wildlife. So, on this fragile continent at least, dogsledding has reached the end of the trail.

SLED-DOG RACING · Sled dogs may have had their day at the South Pole, but there is no end in sight for sled-dog racers. The sport is fun for everyone everywhere—except in climates too warm for dogs to run. Yearly races take place not only in Alaska, but from Laconia, New Hampshire, to Truckee, California.

Sled-dog races have been held for years—wherever people have felt the urge to race their dogs. Organized dogsled racing began with the 408-mile (656-kilometer) All-Alaska Sweepstakes in 1908. Some races are run according to the rules of the International Sled Dog Racing Association. Other sled-dog clubs go by their own rules. All rules have the dogs' welfare at heart.

Sprint racing is a very popular sport, especially because you don't have to go to the wilderness to participate.

Short "sprint" races and long-distance "endurance" races are the most popular kinds of contests.

Sprint racing. In sprint races, dog teams (classed in groups of three, five, seven, and seven-to-sixteen dogs) race anywhere from 3 to 30 miles (5 to 50 kilometers), depending on the size of the team.

Many children (from about age six up) and their dogs take part in junior sled-dog sprint races. One favorite is the Anchorage Fur Rendezvous Alascom Junior World Championship—better known as part of the "Fur Rondy," in which adults also race. Another junior competition is the All American Championship Sled Dog Races in Ely, Minnesota. Win or lose, mushers and dogs have a great time. So do onlookers.

Endurance racing. Some endurance races run 250 to 300 miles (400 to 480 kilometers); others much more. One famous race, in 1925, covered almost 700 miles (1,126 kilometers) in 127 hours. This race, however, was not a sports event. It was a desperate mission to get medicine from Nenana, Alaska, to a hospital in Nome to end a diphtheria epidemic.

With temperatures at -50 degrees Fahrenheit (-10 degrees Celsius), sled-dog drivers ran relays, each team taking turns carrying the serum. The trail ran over mountains, across sea ice, and through raging blizzards.

A gray Siberian husky named Togo led Leonhard Seppala's team on the longest leg of the relay, crossing the jagged ice of Norton Bay. Balto, Gunnar Kaasen's strong black Alaskan husky, led another team on the final lap, plowing through deep

Balto and his driver Gunnar Kaasen. Balto became famous
in 1925 when he delivered a lifesaving medicine to Nome,
Alaska, during a diphtheria epidemic.

snowdrifts and finding the way through a blizzard when Kaasen
could not see to steer.

Togo and Balto became famous for their heroic roles in the
race. But it was really because of the skill and stamina of all the
sled dogs and their drivers that the serum reached Nome in time
to save many lives.

Strictly for the challenge of long-distance racing, Alaska's Iditarod Trail Sled Dog Race has been run between Anchorage and Nome every year since 1973. In part, it follows a trail over which mail and supplies were carried to the mining town of Iditarod during Alaska's gold rush in the 1890s and early 1900s.

Teams of seven to eighteen dogs take part. The race is more than 1,000 miles (1,609 kilometers) long and can take anywhere up to four weeks. In 1990, Susan Butcher's team ran the course in 11 days, 53 minutes, and 23 seconds—breaking her own 1986 record of 11 days and 15 hours. Butcher won the Iditarod race four times and set several records on other trails.

You might wonder why—considering the hardships of frigid weather and the hazards of racing—many people devote their lives to dogsledding.

Most mushers would tell you: They love the outdoors, especially cold, bracing air. They love the quiet, white countryside. They love the excitement of a good race. But most of all they love the powerful, spirited animals that live and travel with them.

And the dogs? Do they get as big a thrill out of pulling sleds across ice and through snow? Born to run, it certainly looks as if they fully enjoy the sporting life.

Susan Butcher once said: "At the start of a race, the dogs are so anxious to get going, it takes ten people to hold them back as earlier starters move out."

And Nettie Hall (the Michigan musher) once described the end of a long race: "My dogs rolled in the snow, cooling themselves off, but also in the joy of having had a good run."

Dogsledding. What better way for top-notch athletes to work off some steam and make use of their remarkable skills?

A tired husky, his feet cozy in their handmade booties, takes a nap during a break in the Iditarod Trail Sled Dog Race.

FURTHER READING

Casey, Brigid, and Wendy Haugh. *Sled Dogs*. New York: Dodd, Mead, 1983.

Fichter, George. *Working Dogs*. New York: Watts, 1979.

London, Jack. *The Call of the Wild*. Milwaukee, Wis.: Raintree, 1980.

_____. *White Fang*. New York: Scholastic, 1972.

OWL Magazine Editors. *The Kids' Dog Book*. Racine, Wis.: Western, 1984.

Randles, Slim. *Dogsled*. New York: Winchester Press, 1976.

Riddles, Libby, and Tim Jones. *Race Across Alaska*. Harrisburg, Pa.: Stackpole Books, 1988.

INDEX

ABOUT THE AUTHOR

Free-lance writer and editor Elizabeth Ring is a former teacher and editor at *Ranger Rick's Nature Magazine*. Her previous books for children include two biographies, *Rachel Carson: Caring for the Earth* and *Henry David Thoreau: In Step With Nature*, published by The Millbrook Press. Also published by The Millbrook Press are two other books by Elizabeth Ring in the *Good Dogs!* series, *Detector Dogs: Hot on the Scent* and *Assistance Dogs: In Special Service*. She has also written on a range of programs on environmental subjects for the National Wildlife Federation. She lives in Woodbury, Connecticut, with her husband, writer and photographer William Hennefrund. Although five dogs have been a part of the family over the years, three cats are current companions.